U.S. Regions

The People of the
West

Blaine Wiseman

MEDIA ENHANCED BOOKS
AV² BY WEIGL™
ADDED VALUE • AUDIO VISUAL

www.av2books.com

AV² provides enriched content that supplements and complements this book. Weigl's AV² books strive to create inspired learning and engage young minds in a total learning experience.

Your AV² Media Enhanced books come alive with...

Audio
Listen to sections of the book read aloud.

Key Words
Study vocabulary, and complete a matching word activity.

Video
Watch informative video clips.

Quizzes
Test your knowledge.

Go to www.av2books.com, and enter this book's unique code.

BOOK CODE

Y983208

Embedded Weblinks
Gain additional information for research.

Slide Show
View images and captions, and prepare a presentation.

AV² by Weigl brings you media enhanced books that support active learning.

Try This!
Complete activities and hands-on experiments.

... and much, much more!

Published by AV² by Weigl
350 5ᵗʰ Avenue, 59ᵗʰ Floor
New York, NY 10118

Websites: www.av2books.com   www.weigl.com

Library of Congress Control Number: 2014942100

ISBN 978-1-4896-2470-3 (hardcover)
ISBN 978-1-4896-2471-0 (softcover)
ISBN 978-1-4896-2472-7 (single-user eBook)
ISBN 978-1-4896-2473-4 (multi-user eBook)

Printed in the United States of America in North Mankato, Minnesota
1 2 3 4 5 6 7 8 9 18 17 16 15 14

062014
WEP060614

Project Coordinator: Aaron Carr
Design: Mandy Christiansen

Every reasonable effort has been made to trace ownership and to obtain permission to reprint copyright material. The publishers would be pleased to have any errors or omissions brought to their attention so that they may be corrected in subsequent printings.

Weigl acknowledges Getty Images as its primary image supplier for this title.

Contents

Introducing the West

The West is the largest region in the United States. It has always attracted pioneers adventurers, explorers, and **prospectors**. People of the West live among towering mountains, dry deserts, remote islands, freezing tundra, vast prairies, and rocky coastlines. Throughout the region, they have built huge cities and bustling industries. They have used natural resources to not only survive, but thrive. Today, Westerners continue exploring, innovating, and building to make their lives and region better.

Washington
Oregon
Montana
Idaho
Wyoming
Nevada
Utah
California
Colorado
Arizona
New Mexico
Pacific Ocean
MEXICO

Legend
- ■ West (11 states)
- □ Southwest (5 states)
- □ Northeast (11 states)
- ■ Southeast (11 states)
- ▨ Midwest (12 states)

Alaska
0   500 Miles
0   500 Km

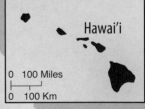

Hawai'i
0   100 Miles
0   100 Km

Where People Live in the West

Compare the populations of the biggest city in each Western state.

City	Population
Los Angeles, **California**	3,857,799
Phoenix, **Arizona**	1,488,750
Seattle, **Washington**	634,535
Portland, **Oregon**	603,106

CANADA

North Dakota

Minnesota

South Dakota

Wisconsin

Lake Superior

Michigan

Lake Huron

Lake Michigan

Iowa

Nebraska

UNITED STATES

Indiana

Ohio

Lake Erie

Lake Ontario

New York

Pennsylvania

New Hampshire

Maine

Vermont

Massachusetts

Rhode Island

Connecticut

New Jersey

Delaware

Maryland

Kansas

Missouri

Illinois

Kentucky

West Virginia

Virginia

Oklahoma

Arkansas

Tennessee

North Carolina

South Carolina

Texas

Mississippi

Alabama

Georgia

Atlantic Ocean

N

Louisiana

Florida

Gulf of Mexico

0 ——— 250 Miles

0 ——— 250 Kilometers

City	Population	City	Population
Las Vegas, **Nevada**	596,424	Salt Lake City, **Utah**	189,314
Honolulu, **Hawai'i**	337,256	Billings, **Montana**	106,954
Anchorage, **Alaska**	298,610	Cheyenne, **Wyoming**	61,537
Boise, **Idaho**	212,303		

*2012 population figures

Settling the West

The West was the last region to join the United States. However, many groups of people lived there long before that. Ancestors of modern American Indians moved from Asia to Alaska, and then throughout North America. They settled in different places all over the continent and developed unique cultures. In the West, there were groups such as the Hopi, Navajo, Aleut, Chippewa, and many others. Meanwhile, Hawai'ians built a culture isolated from others by the vast ocean surrounding them.

The traditional ways of **indigenous** American Indian and Hawai'ian peoples were changed forever when Europeans arrived in the West. The first Europeans in the region were explorers. They came alone or in small groups, but many more would soon follow. As the whole country grew, millions of people made their way West, seeking a new way of life.

Western Migrations

13,000 BC
During the last ice age, Alaska was connected to Asia by a piece of land that is now under water. Following herds of mammals, ancient tribes **migrated** to this area into North America. These were the first Americans.

AD 200–500
The first Hawai'ians spent months crossing the ocean in special canoes. They came from Polynesia, more than 2,000 miles (3,200 km) away. They would live on the islands of Hawai'i untouched by other cultures for more than 1,000 years.

1800s
Fur traders and explorers followed trails that began in Illinois and went all the way to Oregon. These trails had been used for centuries by American Indians. By the 1840s, large groups of people began to migrate to the West.

1849
When gold was discovered in California, prospectors seeking riches rushed to the West. Small towns grew into big cities such as San Francisco and Sacramento.

1869
As more people moved to the West, transportation became more important. Traveling by wagon was slow and difficult. When the first **transcontinental** railroad was completed, it allowed millions more people to easily reach the West.

Historic Events

Throughout history, the West has been shaped by people and by forces of nature. Explorers have made important discoveries, opening the West to migration and settlement. Wars and conflicts have divided the land, while natural disasters have shown that people are not always in control. All of the major historical events in the region's history have helped shape the region and its people.

Texas 1848 Treaty of Guadalupe Hidalgo
The Mexican-American War began as a dispute over part of Texas. It ended with the signing of the Treaty of Guadalupe Hidalgo. The agreement gave the United States control of Texas, New Mexico, and Colorado, along with the Western states of California, Nevada, Utah, and Arizona.

Arizona and Nevada 1936 Hoover Dam

Many areas of the West are very dry, which makes farming difficult. During the Great Depression, President Hoover decided to help. The Hoover Dam **irrigates** more than 1 million acres (400,000 hectares) of land in the United States. It also provides water to more than 18 million people throughout the West.

Hawai'i 1941 Pearl Harbor

The United States did not want to join World War II, but they were left with no choice. On December 7, 1941, Japanese warplanes attacked the U.S. naval base at Pearl Harbor, Hawai'i. More than 2,400 people were killed. The next day, the U.S. joined the war.

★ The second strongest earthquake ever recorded struck Alaska on March 27, 1964. The quake caused 131 deaths, a great deal of damage to buildings and roads, and powerful **tsunamis** as far away as California.

In 1867, U.S. President Andrew Johnson paid Russia **$7.2 million** for Alaska.

As part of the Treaty of Guadalupe Hidalgo, the U.S. paid Mexico **$15 million.**

Historic Westerners

The West has always been a land that inspires big dreams and big ideas. Throughout history, it has attracted people seeking something different. These explorers, leaders, and artists, helped the West to become well-known and built a stronger region.

Captain James Cook (1728–1779)

By the time Great Britain's Captain James Cook arrived in the West, he had spent years exploring and mapping new lands. In 1778, he became the first European to see Hawai'i. He also went to Oregon, Washington, and Alaska. He was the first European to make contact with American Indians of the northwest coast.

★ Captain Cook explored and mapped Australia and New Zealand, and spent many years looking for Antarctica.

Meriwether Lewis (1774–1809) and William Clark (1770–1838)

From 1803 to 1806, Lewis and Clark's Corps of Discovery traveled from Missouri to the coast of Oregon. They paddled through raging rivers and crossed the Rocky Mountains on horseback. Along the way, they made many important discoveries.

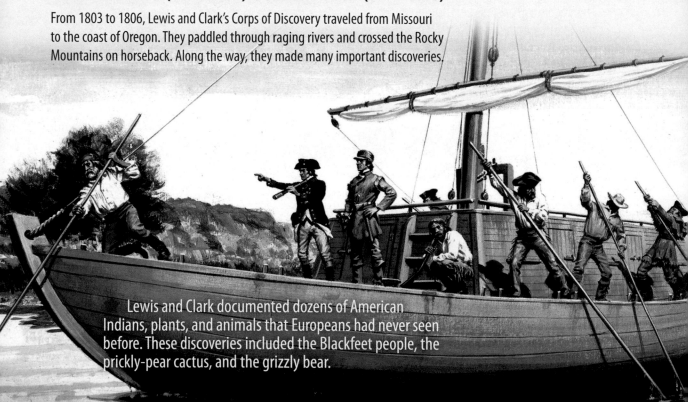

Lewis and Clark documented dozens of American Indians, plants, and animals that Europeans had never seen before. These discoveries included the Blackfeet people, the prickly-pear cactus, and the grizzly bear.

Geronimo (1829–1909)

Geronimo was a chief of the Apache people when the United States expanded into the West. He fought for his people and for their land. When the U.S. took over the territory, they forced the Apache onto **reservations**. Geronimo led his people to escape from the reservations and continue their traditional lifestyles.

Queen Lydia Liliuokalani (1838–1917)

Queen Liliuokalani was the last **monarch** of Hawai'i. In 1893, she wrote a new **constitution** that would have given native Hawai'ians more power over their islands. United States' troops surrounded her palace and overthrew the Queen. While Queen Liliuokalani fought for her peoples' rights, the U.S. took full control of the islands in 1898.

Charles M. Russell (1864–1926)

Charles M. Russell moved to the West when he was 16. In Montana, he studied the lives of American Indian peoples. During his spare time, he painted the scenes he saw on the frontier. In total, Russell created about 4,000 works of art. His detailed paintings tell the story of traditional life in the West.

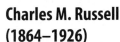

Ansel Adams (1902–1984)

Born in San Francisco, California, Ansel Adams struggled in school, but studied photography in his own time. Adams became popular for his black and white photographs of Yosemite National Park and other natural areas in the West.

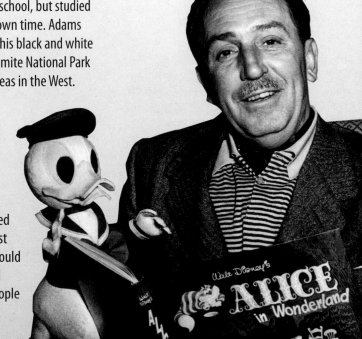

Walt Disney (1901–1966)

In 1928, Walt Disney released the first cartoon with sound. This cartoon introduced Mickey Mouse, now one of the world's most well-known characters. Many more hits would follow. Today, Disney's films, cartoons, and theme parks continue to be enjoyed by people all over the world.

Cultural Groups

A diverse mix of cultural groups call the West home. The majority of the population in the region is descended from Europeans. This is especially true in states such as Montana, Idaho, Wyoming, Utah, and Alaska. Chinese-Americans also played a major role in settling the West. They now live all over the region. Large communities, or *barrios*, of Hispanic people have been established in California and Arizona. In Hawai'i, the native Hawai'ian population mixes with large populations of European, Japanese, and Filipino descent. Many of these groups still practice their own cultural traditions.

★ People all over the world celebrate Chinese New Year with street parades and dragon dances. In Chinese culture, dragons are believed to bring good luck.

Cultural Communities

All over the West, cultural groups live in communities where they speak their native languages and carry on their unique cultural practices.

Koreatown, Los Angeles, California

In the 1970s, a large number of people **immigrated** to the United States from Korea and settled in Los Angeles. These immigrants built new lives for themselves in an area that became known as Koreatown. Korean restaurants, shops, and other businesses give a unique flavor to this part of L.A.

East Los Angeles, California

A large Mexican population has lived in the Los Angeles area since before the Mexican-American War. In the 1910s, during the Mexican Revolution, many more immigrants arrived, settling in the same area. Today, East Los Angeles is the largest Hispanic community in the United States.

Salt Lake City, Utah

In 1846, the followers of the Mormon church decided to head West. Following the Oregon Trail for much of the journey, they eventually ended up at the Great Salt Lake. At first, 1,600 Mormons made the trek, but many more followed. Today, about 60 percent of Utah's population are Mormons.

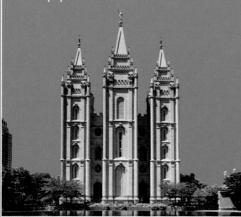

Chinatown, Seattle, Washington

In the 1880s, thousands of Chinese people worked on railroads, in mines, and in factories, helping develop the West. In Seattle, they settled in an area that became known as Chinatown. Today, Seattle's Chinatown-International District is one of the most diverse neighborhoods in the region.

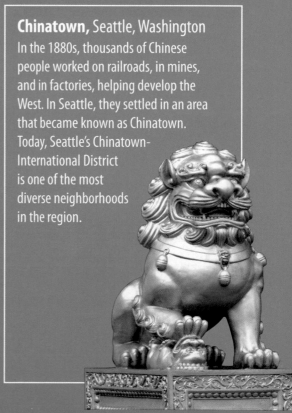

Major Cities of the West

The West is a land of differences. It is home to both the most populated and least populated states in the United States. Some of the biggest and smallest major cities can also be found in the West.

Anchorage is the biggest city in Alaska, containing 40 percent of the population. It did not become a town until 1915, when a railroad was built through Alaska. Then, the population began to grow quickly. New industries were introduced and, in the 1960s, oil was discovered nearby. This discovery attracted many more people to the city.

Los Angeles, California, is the biggest city in the West, and the second biggest city in the United States. Almost 4 million people live in the "City of Angels." The movie industry has made areas such as Hollywood and Beverly Hills well known all over the world.

Phoenix, Arizona, is known as the "Valley of the Sun." The Hohokam people built irrigation canals there, but left the area 600 years ago. The area was not settled again until the 1860s. Today, Phoenix is one of the fastest growing cities in the United States.

Phoenix is named after the mythical bird that rose from the ashes.

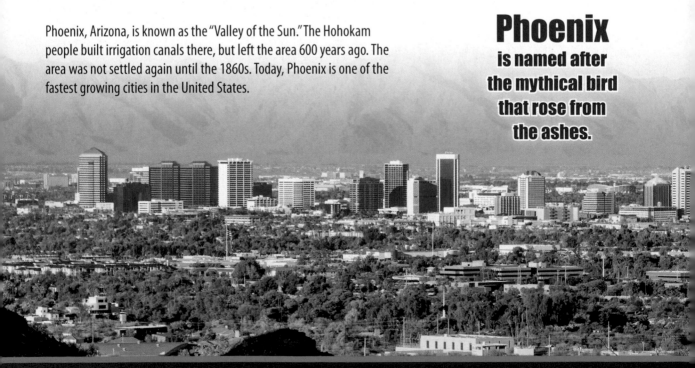

In the 1890s, Seattle, Washington, was a small town. A gold rush more than 1,000 miles (1,600 km) north, however, turned it into a major city. Prospectors flocked to the Klondike region in Canada, sailing north from Seattle. Today, Seattle is a major manufacturing center, and home to many different industries. It is known as "The Emerald City."

State Capitals

A state capital is an important city because this is where the state government is based. The government's leaders work in the capital, making major decisions that impact the whole state on local, regional, national, and international levels.

State Capitals	Population
Phoenix, **Arizona**	**1,488,750**
Sacramento, **California**	**475,516**
Honolulu, **Hawai'i**	**337,256**
Boise, **Idaho**	**212,303**
Salt Lake City, **Utah**	**189,314**
Salem, **Oregon**	**154,637**
Cheyenne, **Wyoming**	**61,537**
Carson City, **Nevada**	**54,838**
Olympia, **Washington**	**46,478**
Juneau, **Alaska**	**32,556**
Helena, **Montana**	**29,134**

*2012 population figures

Industries of the West

The West has many natural resources in its wide open spaces. This allows for a great deal of different industries. People have used the region's land and resources for agriculture, mining, forestry, fishing, and oil. These industries provide the people of the West with jobs and money. They attract more people to the region every year.

Hawai'i

Tourism is Hawai'i's biggest industry. About 7 million people visit the state every year.

- **145,235 jobs**
- Tourists spend about **$12.5 billion per year** in Hawai'i.

Idaho

Idaho produces about one-third of the potatoes in the United States.

- **12 billion pounds (5.4 billion kg) per year**
- **$2.7 billion per year**

Wyoming

Agriculture brings $1 billion to Wyoming's economy every year. Beef is the largest product of the industry. There are more than twice as many cattle as people in Wyoming.

- **1.3 million cattle compared to 582,658 people**
- **$600 million per year**

Alaska

The oil industry creates one-third of Alaska's jobs and about 90 percent of its income.

- **110,000 jobs**
- **$6 billion per year**

Arizona

Copper mining is one of Arizona's biggest industries. The state produces 68 percent of the country's copper.

- **49,800 jobs**

- Arizonans earn **$3.2 billion per year** from copper.

California

California's technology industry is one of the biggest in the country. Internet, gaming, and computer companies lead the way.

- **968,800 jobs**

- The industry pays about **$120 billion** to its workers every year.

Washington

Washington has grown into one of the United States' major manufacturing states. Shipbuilding and airplane manufacturing are some of the largest industries.

- **257,600 jobs**
- **$37.5 billion per year**

Utah

Cows are important to Utah, and dairy farming makes up a large part of the economy.

- **163 million pounds (73.9 million kilograms)** of milk produced in 2012
- **90,000 dairy cows in Utah**

Oregon

While other states rely on the oil industry, Oregon is the nation's leader in renewable energy. Wind and wave power are important parts of this industry.

- **68,709 jobs**

- More than **$2 billion** has been invested in renewable energy to date.

Nevada

The entertainment industry creates nearly 25 percent of jobs in Nevada. Almost eight percent of all overseas visitors to the United States travel to Las Vegas.

- **386,181 jobs**

- The average entertainment worker in Nevada earns **$36,656 per year.**

Western Tourism

The well-known natural areas and bustling big cities of the West attract millions of visitors each year. The West is home to some of the most popular tourist attractions in the United States. These include national parks and amusement parks.

California Disneyland covers 500 acres (167 hectares) of land in Anaheim, California. Since it opened in 1955, 600 million visitors have explored "The Happiest Place on Earth."

Alaska Alaska's Denali National Park is home to the tallest mountain in the United States. Mount McKinley is 20,320 feet (6,200 meters) tall. The chance to see rare wildlife such as grizzly bears and wolves along the park's hiking trails helps attract about 400,000 visitors every year.

Wyoming In 1872, President Ulysses S. Grant made Yellowstone the world's first national park. Approximately 96 percent of it is in Wyoming, but it also reaches into Montana and Idaho. Each year, about 3 million people visit the park to see 67 species of mammals and more than 300 **geysers**.

Arizona The Grand Canyon was carved into the Arizona desert over millions of years by the Colorado River. It measures 277 miles (445 km) long, 18 miles (29 km) across at its widest point, and averages about 1 mile (1.6 km) deep. Grand Canyon National Park is home to five American Indian groups and attracts almost 5 million visitors each year.

Montana At Montana's border with Canada, Glacier National Park is joined with Canada's Waterton Lakes National Park. Together, they form the world's first International Peace Park. Glacier is home to 25 glaciers, 700 miles (1,127 km) of hiking trails, and the Going-to-the-Sun Road. The park's spectacular views attract around 2 million visitors every year.

Oregon With a depth of 1,943 feet (592 m), Crater Lake is the deepest lake in the United States. The crater that the lake lies in is actually a volcano. There are no rivers to feed or drain the lake, so all of its water comes from rain and snowfall. Almost 500,000 people visit the shimmering blue lake every year.

Hawai'i Almost half of the people who died in the attack on Pearl Harbor were sailors on the USS *Arizona*. Today, a memorial sits over top of the sunken battleship and the remains of more than 1,000 U.S. sailors. Every year, more than 1 million people visit the memorial.

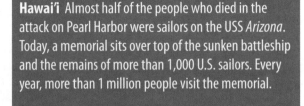

Denali gets its name from an Athabascan Indian word that means **"The High One."**

It took **500 years** of rain and snow to fill Crater Lake.

Famous Westerners

While fame seekers flock to Hollywood, the West has produced many famous athletes, public servants, and actors as well.

Bill Gates grew up in Seattle and began programming computers when he was 13. In 1975, he started his own company, Microsoft. It became the biggest software company in the world. In 2000, he and his wife, Melinda, donated $28 billion to start a charity that spreads education and health around the world.

Bill Gates is the world's richest person, worth more than $77 billion.

Steve Jobs grew up in Silicon Valley, California. Jobs and his father would often work on electronics in their garage. This hobby helped Jobs start his first company, Apple Computers, when he was 21. The company grew to become one of the largest computer companies in the world, creating innovative products such as the iPod and iPhone.

Steve Jobs also owned Pixar, the studio that made movies such as Toy Story, Cars, Finding Nemo, *and* Up.

San Diego, California's **Shaun White** was skateboarding and snowboarding by the age of 6. When he was only 19, White won his first Olympic gold medal, and added a second four years later. White has also won a record 14 gold medals at the X Games, competing in both skateboarding and snowboarding events.

Sandra Day O'Connor

grew up in Arizona. After working as a lawyer, O'Connor became state senator in Arizona. She later became a judge. In 1981, she became the first female Justice of the U.S. Supreme Court. In 2009, O'Connor was awarded the Presidential Medal of Freedom. This medal is awarded by the president each year to people who make an outstanding contribution to society.

Miranda Cosgrove was

born in Los Angeles in 1993. She became well known for her roles in the movie *School of Rock* and TV shows such as *Drake & Josh*. In 2007, Cosgrove got her biggest break, playing the lead role on the hit show, *iCarly*. In this, she was able to show off both her acting and musical talents. Today, she is a rising star in TV, movies, and music.

Venus and Serena Williams

were born one year apart and grew up in Compton, California. In high school, the sisters became professional tennis players. Since then, they have dominated the sport. Serena has won 23 Grand Slam tournaments, while Venus has won 7. They have each won four Olympic gold medals, winning three together as doubles partners.

Born in Los Angeles, **Angelina Jolie** has become famous for playing strong female characters. She won an Oscar in 1999. Besides acting, Jolie has become a strong supporter of human rights. She has worked for the United Nations (UN), helping **refugees** in war torn regions such as Darfur, Sudan. In 2005, the UN gave her the Global Humanitarian Action Award for her work with refugees.

Leonardo DiCaprio

was born in Los Angeles where he loved acting and performing skits with his parents. As a child, he got a few small roles on TV shows, and eventually began starring in movies. DiCaprio has worked with legendary directors, and starred in some of the most successful movies of all time, such as *Titanic*.

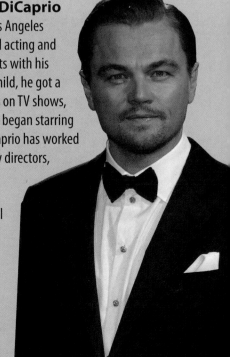

Western Politics

People in the West have many different political views. The policies of politicians can affect a state, the entire region, or even the whole country. Both major parties are represented in the West. Western politicians have had a major impact on the United States.

Born in Hawai'i and raised in California, Barack Obama became the first African-American President in 2008. During his presidency, Obama has ended wars in Iraq and Afghanistan, and introduced the Affordable Health Care Act.

Ronald Reagan was a successful actor before he became the governor of California. Known as "The Great Communicator," he became President in 1981. Reagan helped end the **Cold War** and pulled the United States out of an **economic recession**.

Richard Nixon was born in Yorba Linda, California. After serving as a congressman, senator, and vice president, Nixon became president. He helped end **segregation** in schools, and built working relationships with China and the **Soviet Union**. In 1974, Nixon became the only President to **resign**.

Arnold Schwarzenegger was the best-known action movie star in the world when he became governor of California. The former Mr. Universe and star of *The Terminator* movies won two elections, serving as governor for eight years.

Before he entered politics, John McCain was a war hero. During the Vietnam War, his plane was shot down, and McCain was taken prisoner and tortured for six years. After the war, he became a congressman and senator in Arizona. In 2008, McCain ran for president. He lost to Barack Obama.

State Politics

In the 2012 presidential election, Western states were split between the two major political parties. Red states mostly voted for the Republican Party, while blue states supported the Democratic Party.

Legend
- (R)—Republican
- (D)—Democratic

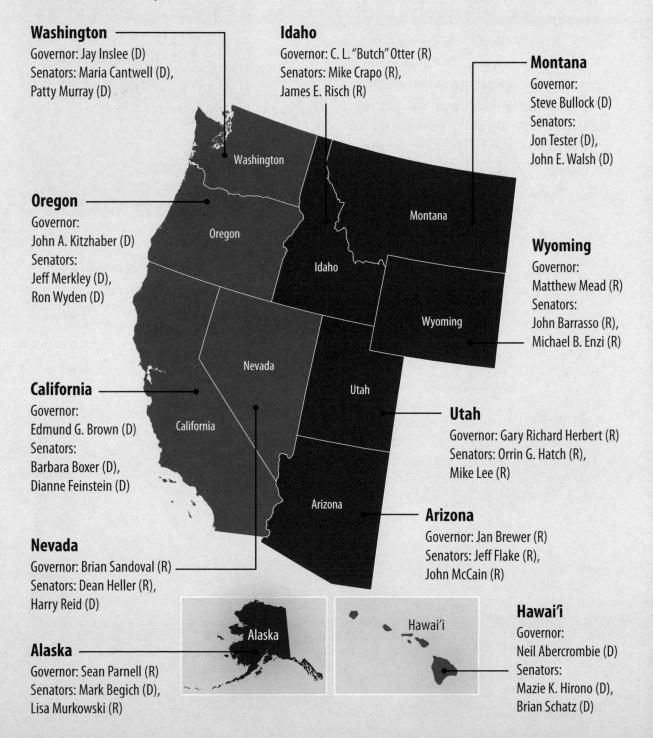

Washington
Governor: Jay Inslee (D)
Senators: Maria Cantwell (D), Patty Murray (D)

Idaho
Governor: C. L. "Butch" Otter (R)
Senators: Mike Crapo (R), James E. Risch (R)

Montana
Governor: Steve Bullock (D)
Senators: Jon Tester (D), John E. Walsh (D)

Oregon
Governor: John A. Kitzhaber (D)
Senators: Jeff Merkley (D), Ron Wyden (D)

Wyoming
Governor: Matthew Mead (R)
Senators: John Barrasso (R), Michael B. Enzi (R)

California
Governor: Edmund G. Brown (D)
Senators: Barbara Boxer (D), Dianne Feinstein (D)

Utah
Governor: Gary Richard Herbert (R)
Senators: Orrin G. Hatch (R), Mike Lee (R)

Arizona
Governor: Jan Brewer (R)
Senators: Jeff Flake (R), John McCain (R)

Nevada
Governor: Brian Sandoval (R)
Senators: Dean Heller (R), Harry Reid (D)

Alaska
Governor: Sean Parnell (R)
Senators: Mark Begich (D), Lisa Murkowski (R)

Hawai'i
Governor: Neil Abercrombie (D)
Senators: Mazie K. Hirono (D), Brian Schatz (D)

Monuments and Buildings

The big dreams of Westerners have produced some of the United States' most recognizable buildings and monuments. These amazing feats of engineering challenged the builders to work both with and against the forces of nature. These structures are well known all over the world. They make the West an exciting place to visit.

The Las Vegas Strip is a 4-mile (6.4-km) section of Las Vegas Boulevard. Since the 1940s, the Strip has been the place where Las Vegas' giant hotels and casinos have been built. Many hotels feature replicas of attractions from other cities and other countries such as the Statue of Liberty and the Eiffel Tower .

Golden Gate Bridge is named after the strait at the entrance to San Francisco Bay. The 4,200 foot (129 m) long "International Orange" bridge was the longest in the world when it opened in 1937. Since then, more than 2 billion cars have crossed the bridge.

The Hoover Dam is located 30 miles (48 km) outside of Las Vegas at Black Canyon. It holds back the Colorado River. The dam was built during the Great Depression by 21,000 workers. It stands 726 feet (221 m) high and 1,244 feet (379 m) across. At the time, it was the government's biggest construction project ever.

When Seattle's Space Needle was built for the 1962 World's Fair, it was the tallest building west of the Mississippi River. Standing 605 feet (184 m) tall, the tower is visited by more than 2.5 million people every year.

Around 750 years ago, ancestors of modern Pueblo Indians built communities in the cliffs of northeast Arizona. At the Navajo National Monument, hundreds of houses and other buildings still stand. The Pueblo ancestors farmed there, but were forced to leave when a long drought dried up the soil.

On top of Hawai'i's tallest mountain, some of the world's largest telescopes look deep into space. The Mauna Kea Observatories are a series of 13 telescopes 4,205 feet (1,282 m) above the sea. At this altitude, there are no clouds or light pollution, making it one of the best places in the world for **astronomy**.

Flags and Seals

Flags and seals are used to show important symbols of a state. State flags are flown above important buildings and monuments. They are used to claim ownership of a place. Seals help represent a state's history, its industries, and its values. They are used on government documents, letters, and memos. Many states also use the seal on the front of their state flag.

California

Flag The grizzly bear stands for strength and the star represents sovereignty, the authority to govern itself.

Seal The 31 stars show that California was the 31st state in the Union. The grizzly bear and grapes represent the nature and agriculture of the region.

Oregon

Flag Oregon's flag is blue and gold—the official state colors, and 1859 is the year Oregon joined the Union.

Seal There are 33 stars on the seal, showing that Oregon was the 33rd state in the Union. The wheat, plow, and pickax represent agriculture and mining.

Arizona

Flag The copper star stands for the copper industry and the 13 beams represent the 13 original colonies of the United States.

Seal The sun rising behind mountains represents the beauty of the region, and 1912 is the year Arizona joined the Union.

Wyoming

Flag Bison is the state's official animal. Red, white, and blue are the colors of the United States.

Seal 1869 is the year a government was organized in the territory, and 1890 is the year Wyoming became a state. The woman in the middle holding an "Equal Rights" banner stands for liberty and equality; the cowboy represents the cattle industry; the miner represents the mining industry.

Hawai'i

Flag The colors and Union Jack of the British flag show that many of King Kamehameha's advisors were British. Eight stripes represent the eight Hawai'ian islands.

Seal 1959 is the year Hawai'i became the 50th state. King Kamehameha is represented as he united the islands as one kingdom.

Alaska

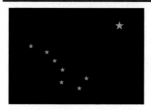

Flag Its blue background stands for the sky, the sea, the lakes, and the alpine forget-me-not, which is the official wildflower of the state. The Big Dipper (Great Bear constellation) is a symbol of strength, and Polaris (the North Star) shows the state's northern location.

Seal The light above the mountains stands for the Northern Lights, and the other symbols show industry—forestry, farming, seafood, and agriculture.

Nevada

Flag The words *Battle Born* indicate that Nevada joined the Union during the Civil War. Silver (star) and blue (background) are the official state colors.

Seal The seal shows a quartz mill and silver mining, which represents the state's wealthy mineral industry. Nevada was the 36th state in the Union—there are 36 stars on the seal.

Idaho

Flag The flag features the official state seal above a red band with the words "State of Idaho".

Seal The woman represents justice, liberty, and equality. The miner represents industry.

Utah

Flag The flag shows the state seal on a blue background. The word *Industry* is the state motto.

Seal The beehive in the center stands for hard work and industry. The two dates are 1847—the year the Mormons arrived in Utah, and 1896—the year Utah joined the Union.

Montana

Flag The flag shows the state seal on a blue background.

Seal The natural beauty of Montana is shown by images of the sunrise over mountains, waterfalls on the Missouri River, hills, trees, and cliffs. The pick, shovel, and plow stand for the mining and farming industries.

Washington

Flag Washington is known as the "Evergreen State." Its flag has the state seal on a green background.

Seal George Washington is the namesake of the state and the first president. 1889 is the year Washington joined the Union.

Challenges Facing the West

Cleaning It Up

Los Angeles has battled problems with air pollution since the early 1900s. The pollution grew worse as the city grew larger. More people meant more cars on the roads. Today, the city has the worst traffic in the United States. Millions of cars sit in traffic jams every day. Each of these vehicles releases **carbon dioxide** into the atmosphere, causing air pollution. This can cause many serious health problems, such as asthma and cancer.

Between the 1940s and 1980s, the **smog** problem grew so bad that the government had to do something about it. In 1984, the California Smog Check program started. Under the program, vehicles have to be checked to make sure they were causing as little pollution as possible. Thanks to the Smog Check program and other laws and programs such as the Clean Air Act, California is cleaning up its air and air pollution is dropping.

Each year, the average Los Angeles resident wastes **59 hours** in traffic.

If a volcano is active, ash, gas, and hot lava can escape from its opening.

Shaking It Up

The west coast and Hawai'i are found in the Ring of Fire, an area around the Pacific Ocean where most of Earth's volcanoes are located. The volcanoes are caused by movement under the surface, the same movement that causes earthquakes. Thousands of earthquakes strike the West every year. While most are too weak to be felt by people, the region has been struck by major quakes throughout history.

In 1906, an earthquake measuring 7.8 on the **Richter Scale** struck San Francisco. Many buildings in the city were not strong enough, and collapsed. Most of the buildings that survived were destroyed by fires that swept through the city after the quake. More than 3,000 people were killed.

The city was rebuilt, but it was not built stronger. Today, the people of San Francisco are trying to fix the problems in case of another earthquake. New buildings must be built to resist earthquakes, and engineers are working to make old buildings and structures stronger.

Parkfield, California, is known as **"The Earthquake Capital of the World."**

Quiz

1 What is the biggest city in Idaho?

2 What is Seattle's nickname?

3 What is the name of America's deepest lake?

4 Where did the first Hawai'ians come from?

5 How much did the United States pay for Alaska?

6 Which Westerner became the first female Supreme Court Justice?

7 Where is America's largest Hispanic community?

9 What two actors became governor of California?

8 Which state produces most of the copper in the United States?

10 Which state's flag and seal feature a beehive?

ANSWERS: 1. Boise 2. The Emerald City 3. Crater Lake 4. Polynesia 5. $7.2 million 6. Sandra Day O'Connor 7. East Los Angeles 8. Arizona 9. Ronald Reagan and Arnold Schwarzenegger 10. Utah

Key Words

astronomy: the study of space and the universe

carbon dioxide: a gas produced by cars

Cold War: a conflict that caused tension between the United States and the then Soviet Union between 1945 and 1989–1991

constitution: a set of rules

economic recession: a downturn in business activities that lasts for an extended time

geysers: geological features that spew hot water from underground into the air

immigrated: came to live in a foreign country

indigenous: originally living in an area

irrigates: uses water to help grow crops

migrated: moved from one area to another

monarch: king or queen

prospectors: people looking for minerals such as gold, silver, or copper

refugees: people who have been forced to leave their home by war or other disaster

reservations: places where American Indians were sent to live by the government

resign: step down or quit a job

Richter Scale: a scale for measuring the strength of an earthquake that ranges from 1 (being the weakest) to 10 (being the strongest)

segregation: to keep two things apart; forcing children of different color to go to different schools

smog: thick air pollution or "smoky fog"

Soviet Union: a former large country in Europe that divided into smaller countries in 1991

transcontinental: crossing the entire continent

tsunamis: massive, destructive ocean waves usually caused by an earthquake

Index

Log on to www.av2books.com

AV² by Weigl brings you media enhanced books that support active learning. Go to www.av2books.com, and enter the special code found on page 2 of this book. You will gain access to enriched and enhanced content that supplements and complements this book. Content includes video, audio, weblinks, quizzes, a slide show, and activities.

AV² Online Navigation

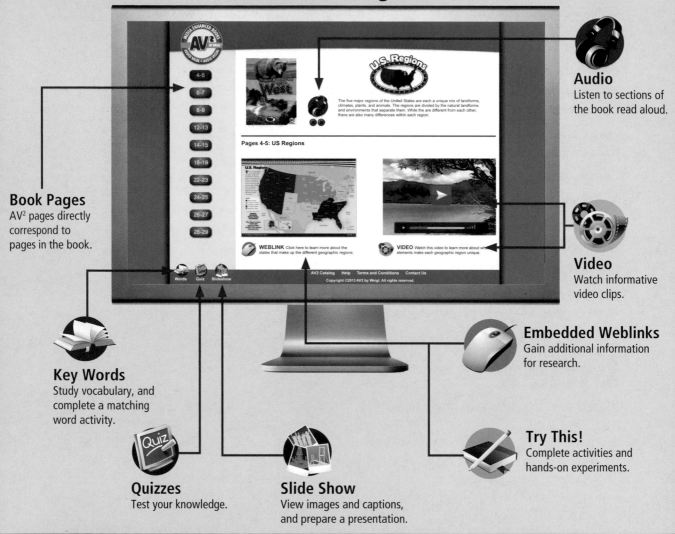

Audio
Listen to sections of the book read aloud.

Book Pages
AV² pages directly correspond to pages in the book.

Video
Watch informative video clips.

Key Words
Study vocabulary, and complete a matching word activity.

Embedded Weblinks
Gain additional information for research.

Try This!
Complete activities and hands-on experiments.

Quizzes
Test your knowledge.

Slide Show
View images and captions, and prepare a presentation.

AV² was built to bridge the gap between print and digital. We encourage you to tell us what you like and what you want to see in the future.

Sign up to be an AV² Ambassador at www.av2books.com/ambassador.